curious about

DUCK HUNTING

BY RACHEL GRACK

AMICUS LEARNING

What are you

CHAPTER ONE
Hunting Basics
PAGE
4

CHAPTER TWO
Get Ready
PAGE
10

curious about?

CHAPTER THREE

Go Hunt

PAGE
18

Stay Curious! Learn More . . . 22
Glossary 24
Index 24

Curious about is published by
Amicus Learning, an imprint of Amicus
P.O. Box 227
Mankato, MN 56002
www.amicuspublishing.us

Editor: Alissa Thielges
Series Designer: Kathleen Petelinsek
Book Designer: Aubrey Harper

Library of Congress Cataloging-in-Publication Data
Names: Koestler-Grack, Rachel A., 1973- author.
Title: Curious about duck hunting / by Rachel Grack.
Description: Mankato, Minnesota: Amicus Learning, an imprint of Amicus, [2024] | Series: Curious about the great outdoors | Includes bibliographical references and index. | Audience: Ages 5–9 | Audience: Grades 2–3 | Summary: "Questions and answers give kids the fundamentals of duck hunting, including what gear to pack and hunting safety. Includes infographics to support visual learning and back matter to support research skills, plus a glossary and index"—Provided by publisher.
Identifiers: LCCN 2023009427 (print) | LCCN 2023009428 (ebook) | ISBN 9781645496601 (library binding) | ISBN 9781681529493 (paperback) | ISBN 9781645496861 (pdf)
Subjects: LCSH: Duck shooting—Juvenile literature.
Classification: LCC SK333.D8 .K64 2024 (print) | LCC SK333.D8 (ebook) | DDC 799.2/44—dc23/eng/20230504
LC record available at https://lccn.loc.gov/2023009427
LC ebook record available at https://lccn.loc.gov/2023009428

Photo credits: Alamy/McClatchy-Tribune, 17, USFWS, 3; Corbis/FWS, 8–9; Freepik/David Costa Fernandez, 7, 16; iStock/GlobalP, 21, ktatarka, 20, NRA-ILA, 10–11, PavelRodimov, 14–15, saz1977, 18–19, SteveOehlenschlager, 6, timalfordphoto, 12, tomprout, 21; Shutterstock/aaltair, 7, Anna Pozzi - Zoophotos,Cover, 1, artichoke studio, 13, Erik Lam, 21, J Edwards Photography, 18–19, Jim Cumming, 7, Menna, 13, rock ptarmigan, 7, Susan Hodgson, 7

Printed in China

CHAPTER ONE

Why do people hunt ducks?

Most hunters enjoy being in nature. They like watching ducks and studying their movements. Some hunt for sport. They find duck meat tasty. For others, hunting is a fun way to spend time with family and friends.

Duck hunting can be a fun challenge for hunters.

Can you hunt any duck?

Hunters learn how to identify ducks even from far away

No. There are 32 huntable duck **species**. These are divided into three groups. Puddle ducks can be found in almost any **waterfowl habitat**. Diving ducks prefer lakes, rivers, and ocean bays. Sea ducks stick to coastal waters and the Great Lakes.

Popular Hunting Ducks: Nonbreeding Ranges

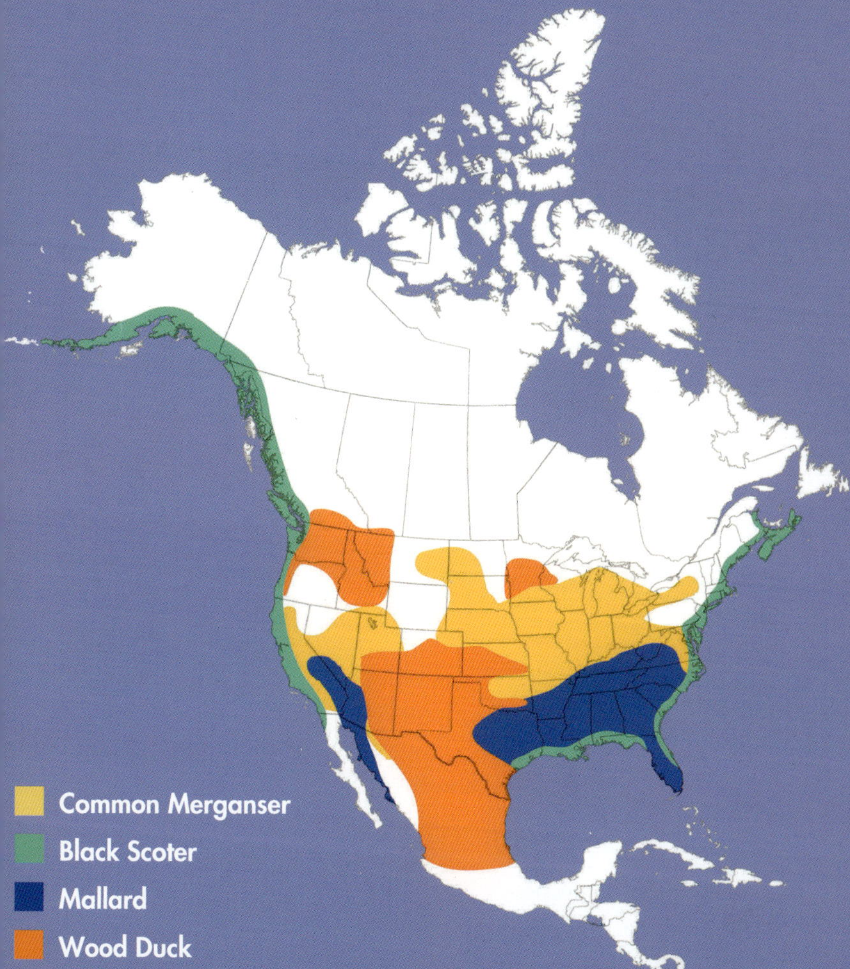

Common Merganser

Black Scoter

Mallard

Wood

When can I hunt?

A hunter takes aim while his dog waits for the signal to fetch.

Duck hunting season opens in early September in the United States and Canada. It ends in December or January. Each state and province has different hunting dates. Be sure to check before you shoot! Many states have waterfowl zones. These may open and close for hunting throughout the year.

CHAPTER TWO

How do you use a gun?

A beginner practices aiming and shooting his gun.

DID YOU KNOW?
If you are 10 or older, you may need a hunting license.

First, take a gun safety class! This teaches you how to handle a gun the right way. It's also important to learn about hunting safety. Many gun clubs have shooting classes for beginners. Kids should use a youth shotgun. These have shorter barrels. A 20-gauge shotgun with light load shells works best.

Clay discs are also called clay pigeons.

Should I practice?

For sure! Many hunters go skeet shooting or trapshooting for practice. In these sports, shooters try to hit moving clay targets. The shooter yells, "Pull!" A round disc launches into the air. The shooter takes aim and fires.

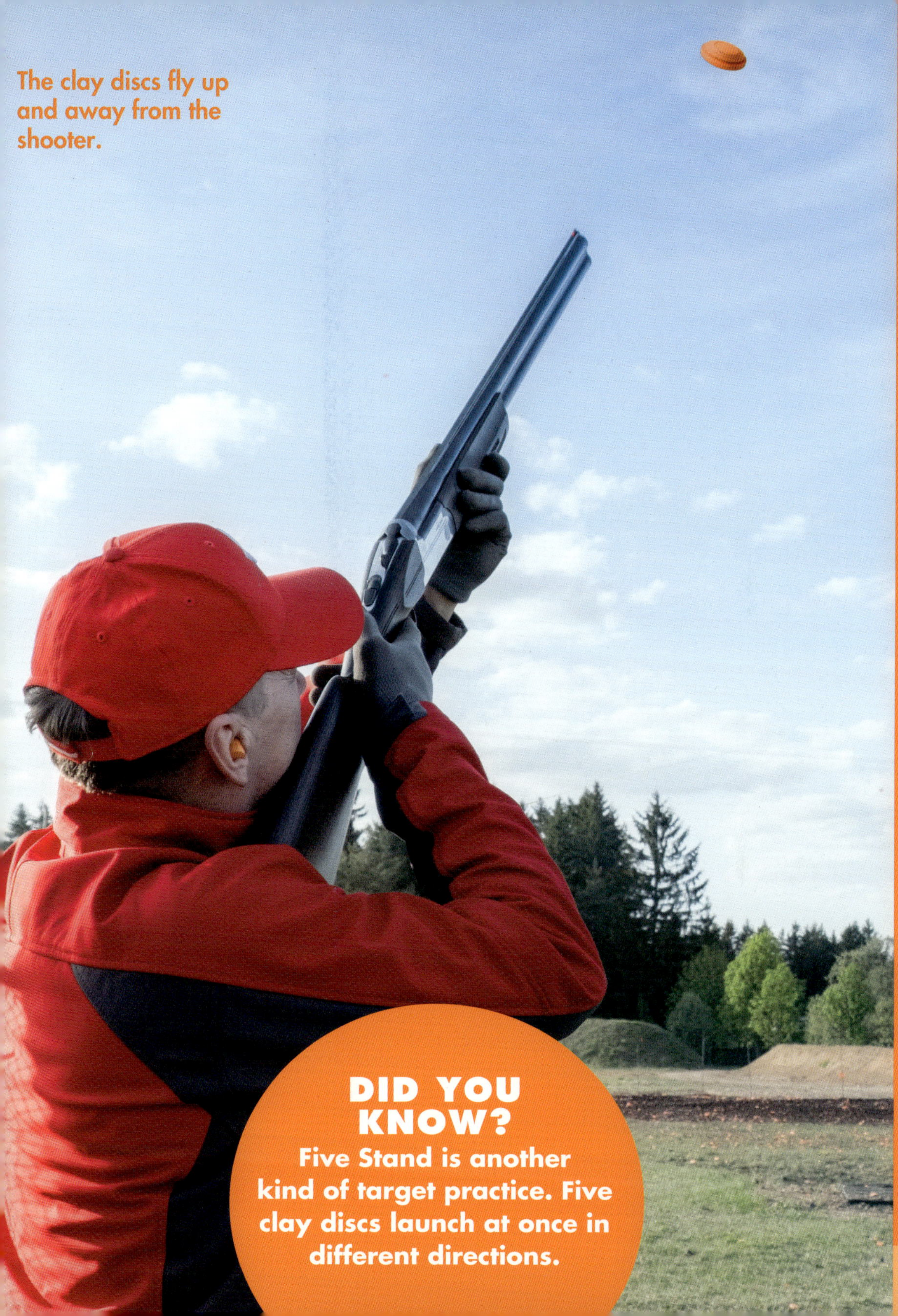

The clay discs fly up and away from the shooter.

DID YOU KNOW?

Five Stand is another kind of target practice. Five clay discs launch at once in different directions.

GET READY

What do I wear?

A hunter wears camouflage head to toe to hide from ducks.

Good question! Duck hunting is often cold and wet. Start with a warm layer like a wool shirt. Hunters often wear waders. These tall rubber boots keep them dry while walking through water. For field hunting, they wear thick overalls. **Camouflage** helps hunters blend into their surroundings.

How do you find ducks?

By **scouting**. Ducks travel along common **flyways**. Hunters watch for ducks on the move. They follow ducks to **roosting** spots. They set up **decoys** when the ducks fly out. Then, they wait in a **blind**. Most hunters use duck calls to draw out birds.

A girl uses a duck call to attract ducks.

CHAPTER THREE

When do I shoot?

This can be tricky! Ducks circle before they land. One might fly right above you. But don't shoot yet. Wait for it to slow down in front of you. It will be easier to hit. Only shoot at ducks within 40 yards (37 meters). That's about the length of two bowling lanes.

Hunters keep both eyes open and aim down the barrel of the gun.

DID YOU KNOW?

It is always safest to hunt with an adult.

I killed one, now what?

Retrievers are easy to train for hunting.

Nice shot! Pay attention to where it drops. Now, go get it. Many hunters use dogs to track and recover birds. Next, **tag** the duck. You can keep hunting. Just stay within the daily **bag limit**. Later, learn how to **clean** your bird. It is ready to cook!

LABRADOR
RETRIEVER

CHESAPEAKE BAY
RETRIEVER

NOVA SCOTIA DUCK
TOLLING RETRIEVER

GERMAN SHORTHAIRED
POINTER

GOLDEN
RETRIEVER

ASK MORE QUESTIONS

How do you clean a duck?

Do I need permission to hunt on someone else's land?

Try a BIG QUESTION: How does duck hunting affect the environment?

SEARCH FOR ANSWERS

Search the library catalog or the Internet.
A librarian, teacher, or parent can help you.

Using Keywords
Find the looking glass.

Keywords are the most important words in your question.

If you want to know about:

- how to clean a duck, type: CLEANING DUCKS
- hunting on private land, type: DUCK HUNTING PERMISSION

LEARN MORE

FIND GOOD SOURCES

Here are some good, safe sources you can use in your research.
Your librarian can help you find more.

Books

Duck Hunting
by Tom Carpenter, 2018.

Go Duck Hunting!
by Lisa M. Bolt Simons, 2022.

Internet Sites

Duck Facts for Kids
http://kiddopedia.net/duck-facts-kids-information-ducks
Kiddopedia is a website with educational videos for kids. Search videos to learn about animals and other topics.

Waterfowl
www.dkfindout.com/us/animals-and-nature/birds/waterfowl
DKFindOut! is an children's educational site with information on many topics. Learn more about waterfowl.

Every effort has been made to ensure that these websites are appropriate for children. However, because of the nature of the Internet, it is impossible to guarantee that these sites will remain active indefinitely or that their contents will not be altered.

SHARE AND TAKE ACTION

Start a family tradition.
Ask an older family member to teach you to hunt. Many families enjoy sharing this time together.

Join a youth hunt.
Check with local duck clubs, and sign up to go hunting with other kids.

Try eating duck meat.
Find a duck hunter and buy a bird. See if you like how duck tastes.

GLOSSARY

bag limit The number ducks that can be killed in a day by law.

blind A hidden shelter to hide duck hunters.

camouflage Coloring or covering that makes it hard to see a hunter.

clean To pluck the feathers and remove the innards of a duck.

decoy A fake duck used to draw in real ducks.

flyway The path of a bird's migration.

roosting Resting.

scouting Looking for something; duck hunters scout for ducks and follow them.

species Kinds of animals.

tag To fill out a tag to put on a duck you shoot; tags include your name, address, and hunting license number.

waterfowl habitat The places where water birds live.

INDEX

bag limits 20
clothing 14–15
decoys 16
duck meat 4, 20
flyways 16
gun safety 11
habitats 7, 16
hunting dogs 20, 21
hunting season 9
scouting 16
shooting 11, 12, 18
skeet shooting 12
species 7
trapshooting 12

About the Author

Rachel Grack has been editing and writing children's books since 1999. She lives in Arizona, a state where the great outdoors offers countless adventures all year long. Horseback riding has been one of her favorite outdoor activities. But geocaching might be her next big adventure.